Goals2Victory

The Planner to Keep You Unstuck and
Realize Your #Goals2Victory

Dr. Shayanna Mungo

BALBOA.PRESS
A DIVISION OF HAY HOUSE

Balboa Press books may be ordered through booksellers or by contacting:

Balboa Press
A Division of Hay House
1663 Liberty Drive
Bloomington, IN 47403
www.balboapress.com
844-682-1282

Print information available on the last page.

ISBN: 979-8-7652-2695-7 (sc)
ISBN: 979-8-7652-2696-4 (e)

Balboa Press rev. date: 05/04/2022

Welcome Page

You have taken time to take action to acknowledge your purpose in life. This is important.

You believe it is possible to continue developing yourself for the greater good of your mission.

This planner is designed to take action and develop behaviors that align with your values and your ideal self. Focus on you for as little as fifteen minutes a day for sustainable self-care habit development.

In this approach, you will establish a foundation to continue habits that are sustainable and receive compounded benefits of reaching your goals.

Why not be better with age?

Paste a picture and write a description of
Your *current self.*
Who are you without naming a title or what you do for a living?

Ideal Self

Who do you know would be a good role model? What is it about how they make you feel that makes you want to mimic their behavior?

As you find a picture or draw below, be thinking about where you would recommend opportunities for others to practice behaving just like your role model. Sometimes it is easier to see a path forward by sharing ideas to others; however, below I will challenge you to take the advice yourself one step at a time. The only opinion that matters is yours, so let's have some fun.

Let's be attached to the idea of taking action more than being perfect.

Paste a picture and build on the description of
your *ideal self.*
Without limits in mind, who could you be?

Later, you will discover how your self-talk (beliefs) would need to evolve to develop a self-talk that will make your ideal self possible. Looking at the list you created. Where can you identify at least one skill that has to be developed or practiced to improve yourself?

Fun Facts

What are some fun facts about you?

_____

_____

_____

_____

What are some fun facts about a person you admire?

_____

_____

_____

_____

What are some feelings that you want to keep experiencing?

_____

_____

_____

_____

Where are some activities that you can participate in this week to experience the feelings you described?

_____

_____

_____

_____

DR. SHAYANNA MUNGO

Thinking Out Loud

There is an area in the human brain where people try to understand what another person is thinking. As humans, the ability to mind-read is still undeveloped. What better way to understand what a person is thinking other than to ask?

This exercise is to ask some people who you trust.

What they think about you (You can ask what they think your superpower is.)

_____

_____

_____

_____

How do you make them feel?

_____

_____

_____

_____

What is the outstanding memory they have of you winning?

_____

_____

_____

_____

Where could you be easier on yourself?

_____

_____

_____

_____

Current Reality

Draw a meme, or tell me about your normal day.

What goals do you achieve from day to day?

_____

_____

_____

_____

Why do you consistently make these kinds of goals?

_____

_____

_____

_____

Which of these goals will support you getting to your ideal self?

_____

_____

_____

_____

DR. SHAYANNA MUNGO

Beliefs

Beliefs are thoughts that you rehearse in your mind. No one has the power to change the things you think about or how often you think about them. You are the master of your mind. Be mindful that you can change what you choose to rehearse on your own schedule.

Write down the recurring thoughts in your head, and accept them as beliefs.

How do these beliefs show up in your current reality?

Ideal Day

Tell me about your ideal day.

_____
_____
_____
_____
_____
_____

What goals do you need to achieve to experience your ideal day?

_____
_____
_____
_____
_____
_____
_____

Why do you think this goal will contribute to making your ideal day possible?

_____
_____
_____
_____
_____
_____
_____

DR. SHAYANNA MUNGO

Develop New Beliefs

Friendly reminder: Beliefs are thoughts that you rehearse in your mind. No one has the power to change the things you think about or how often you think about them. You are the master of your mind. Be mindful that you can change what you choose to rehearse on your own schedule.

It is safe to explore other thoughts. We are going to identify thoughts that are flexible to experience your ideal day.

Write down one to two beliefs that you will develop. You cannot fail. You will simply learn or receive feedback based on your environment and the tools that you have access to. Give yourself grace as you take action and observe the outcome.

How can you intentionally practice rehearsing the new thought? (For example, set an hourly alarm on your phone to edit the alarm name as a verse or statement to break your current routine.)

Importance of Values

Values are your human filter whereby you measure yourself and others based on the standards you hold in high regard. The beliefs you were just identifying play a role in your values. When you practice different thoughts, then you will experience life differently. From that experience, your values and standards will change.

I encourage you to focus on where you can identify experiences to challenge you to explore. Experience speaks louder than words and last in your memory longer.

Below is a limited list of values you can reference on the next section.

Write one value from each experience. Values that you see appear multiple times from different experiences will go in the center box.

accountability	gratitude	recognition
adaptability	growth	respect
authenticity	harmony	responsibility
balance	home	security
belonging	honesty	serenity
collaboration	humor	time
caring	inclusion	tradition
curiosity	independence	trust
dignity	initiative	truth
diversity	justice	uniqueness
equality	knowledge	usefulness
faith	loyalty	vulnerability
family	patience	wisdom
forgiveness	power	youth
grace	pride	

Core Values

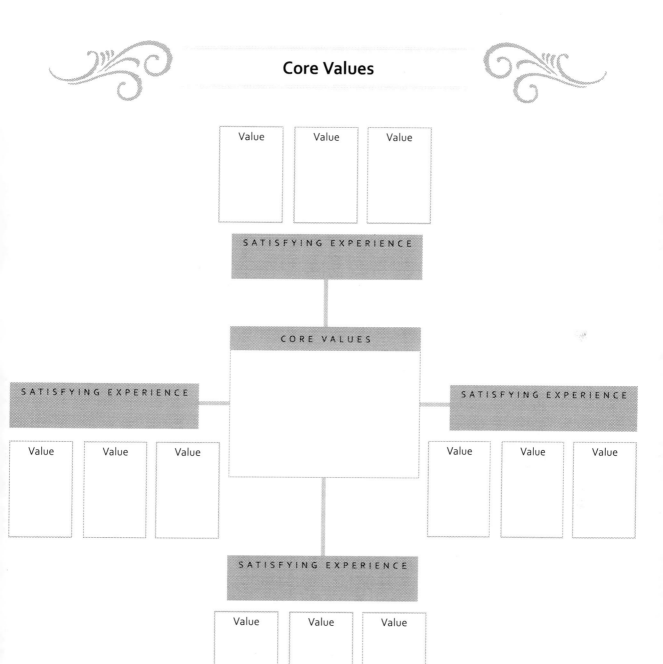

Value · Value · Value

SATISFYING EXPERIENCE

CORE VALUES

SATISFYING EXPERIENCE | SATISFYING EXPERIENCE

Value · Value · Value

Value · Value · Value

SATISFYING EXPERIENCE

Value · Value · Value

Values Challenge

Looking back at your core values, can you identify which values will be challenged when you practice different thoughts?

What values will you develop to be your ideal self?

Why is this important?

DR. SHAYANNA MUNGO

Goal-Setting Work

Write a goal, and then find the real issue to develop against.

Why do you want that for a goal? (Repeat answering this question until there is absolute clarity that there is no other reason to do this goal.) Have you evolved to find the real reason why you never reach your goals?

Individual Example

I want to lose weight because I want to look better. I want to look better because I want to be comfortable in my clothes. I want to look better in my clothes because I believe I will feel more confident. I want to feel confident so that I will lower the likelihood of being rejected. I don't want to be rejected because I don't know how to handle rejection. I want to handle rejection better because I know people will not always agree with me. I want people to agree with me because I know a way to solve problems. What are you doing to cope? This changes the story so I no longer emotionally eat, which aligns to when things don't go my way.

What's the real goal: sharing problem-solving?

What makes you uncomfortable?

What do you do to cope (e.g., emotionally eat) when you are not comfortable?

What will change when you are able to become comfortable?

How to Find the Compounded Results

Identify your behavior (e.g., emotional snacking) when you are coping with not reaching your goal.

Identify the triggers and when. This might include the time of day and the frequency the issue occurs before you must cope.

Example: When people do not agree with me after I have explained multiple times that the next steps in our plan do not make sense, I begin to snack on candy or chips to keep my mouth busy. Otherwise, I may say something awful. I do not want to come across as combative, but I do want to make progress from taking steps that make sense.

Outcome: What Could Accomplishing the Goal Look Like?

Individual Example

When I learn ways to share problem-solving, then I can win by

- sharing success of solving the problem
- reducing the risk of burnout by doing all the work
- reducing the risk of reworking
- not feeling rejected
- feeling confident
- reducing emotional eating
- look and feeling better in my clothes

Microgoals

What is a goal that you have accomplished?

_____

_____

What has accomplishing this goal done for your
- confidence?

  _____

  _____

- family?

  _____

  _____

- community?

  _____

  _____

- finances?

  _____

  _____

- free time?

  _____

  _____

- preparation for your next goal?

  _____

  _____

 # Self-Esteem and Self-Worth Differences

You have your own expectations that you have created. Self-esteem is what you think about yourself. High self-esteem is important because the things you tell yourself about yourself are in your control. The decisions you make are aligned with your self-esteem. Self-esteem is often relative to the job you got, the position you play on a team, or even the degrees that you completed.

Self-worth is not dependent on outside titles. The value in having a high self-worth is you will not need to be validated by others. This is how you feel about yourself. Leading by example requires consistent maintenance on your personal development.

Self-Worth

Are you open to enabling others to support you in reaching your goals? (Examples include taking turns taking a child to practice and patronizing others to help you with chores.)

Think of how responding to that question made you feel.

- Do you have to be in control of a perfect outcome?
- Is your goal worth being sacrificed because of the number of commitments that can be flexible?
- Will you be resentful if your goals are never accomplished? Whose fault will it be?
- Will you avoid making goals if you never achieve them anyway?

DR. SHAYANNA MUNGO

Say this:

- Self, if I do not make myself a priority, then how can I encourage others who look up to me to have an example to follow?

- Self, if I do not tell myself the truth, then why do I get so frustrated when others are lying to me?

- Self, am I tired of being tired yet?

Identify one to two things you are willing to share with a strategy to enable others to develop skills to help you. This list will come easy as soon as you believe you are worth it.

What precommitments do you have that will get in the way of these goals? This goal is worth your effort, so where are some ways to work around your precommitments? Who can you enlist for support to free up time for you for other tasks?

_____

_____

_____

_____

_____

Ground Rules for Power

- Focus on what you want to have happen as opposed to what you don't want to happen.
- Do not try to create or change these rules when you are preoccupied with negative feelings.
- "Knowledge times action equals power" (Jim Kwik).
- "Nearly all men can stand adversity, but if you want to test a man's character, give him power" (Abraham Lincoln).

Rule	Who Needs to Do This	Consequences if Broken
Example: I will not make emotional decisions.	Me	I must ask if there is a way that I can make a change now that I have had time to think about other ways the decision could have been made.
1.		
2.		
3.		
4.		
5.		
6.		
7.		
8.		
9.		
10.		

Distractions

Humans are creatures of habit. This means we have patterns that we follow because of how we keep repeating thoughts that turn into beliefs that turn into values whereby we filter what we allow ourselves to experience.

I want to help you see the patterns that you are open to disrupting to experience a fulfilled life experience, which is described as your ideal day.

Share some distractions that are normalized in your day-to-day that are not serving you well.

_____

_____

_____

_____

_____

_____

Are the distractions stemming from a single or similar cause?

_____

_____

_____

_____

_____

What strengths have you developed to alleviate those distractions?

_____

_____

_____

_____

_____

_____

_____

Resources

List things you tried that didn't work. Which resources can help you get through that hurdle?

List of resources/accountability partners

Name	Email/Website	Phone	Comments/Referral

The next sections are 100 days broken up into 5 sections to track your efforts. The micro goals are tiny goals that will align to your larger goal. Be committed to the change in habits you are developing. Notice the modifications you needed to make to get there more than focus on only achieving your goal with a single strategy.

Day 1

Curiosity

"Nothing is permanent. Don't stress yourself too much
because no matter how bad the situation is, it will change" (unknown).

Microgoal: _____
_____
_____

Trigger forecast: _____
_____
_____

Your mantra: _____
_____
_____

Where do you see value in yourself today? _____
_____
_____

What skill have you sharpened today? _____
_____
_____

I must develop a new habit of _____so that _____
will benefit from my transformation. Developing this new behavior will enable me to live my
ideal day.

Your commitment signature: _____

PS: Lying to yourself teaches others that you will accept their lies too. You owe this to yourself.

Deepen Your Experience

For days 2–20, build on moments that stood out to you as you overcame events that usually trigger you into an old habit.

Activity	Anticipated feeling (At first, I thought …)	Actual feeling (The outcome was unexpected because …)
1.		
2.		
3.		
4.		
5.		
6.		
7.		
8.		
9.		
10.		

Describe the conditions that played a role in your experience. (Was it a once-in-a-lifetime experience?)

_____

_____

_____

_____

Tell me about some patterns you noticed, such as if people are more willing to support you or if people withdraw.

_____

_____

_____

_____

DR. SHAYANNA MUNGO

Day 2

Curiosity

Microgoal: _____

_____

_____

Trigger forecast: _____

_____

_____

Your mantra: _____

_____

_____

Where do you see value in yourself today? _____

_____

_____

What skill have you sharpened today? _____

_____

_____

I must develop a new habit of _____ so that _____ will benefit from my transformation. Developing this new behavior will enable me to live my ideal day.

Your commitment signature: _____

PS: Lying to yourself teaches others that you will accept their lies too. You owe this to yourself.

Day 3

Curiosity

Microgoal: _____
_____
_____

Trigger forecast: _____
_____
_____

Your mantra: _____
_____
_____

Where do you see value in yourself today? _____
_____
_____

What skill have you sharpened today? _____
_____
_____

I must develop a new habit of _____ so that _____ will benefit from my transformation. Developing this new behavior will enable me to live my ideal day.

Your commitment signature: _____

PS: Lying to yourself teaches others that you will accept their lies too. You owe this to yourself.

Day 4

Curiosity

Microgoal: _____
_____
_____

Trigger forecast: _____
_____
_____

Your mantra: _____
_____
_____

Where do you see value in yourself today? _____
_____
_____

What skill have you sharpened today? _____
_____
_____

I must develop a new habit of _____ so that _____ will benefit from my transformation. Developing this new behavior will enable me to live my ideal day.

Your commitment signature: _____

PS: Lying to yourself teaches others that you will accept their lies too. You owe this to yourself.

Day 5

Curiosity

Microgoal: _____
_____
_____

Trigger forecast: _____
_____
_____

Your mantra: _____
_____
_____

Where do you see value in yourself today? _____
_____
_____

What skill have you sharpened today? _____
_____
_____

I must develop a new habit of _____so that _____
will benefit from my transformation. Developing this new behavior will enable me to live my ideal day.

Your commitment signature: _____

PS: Lying to yourself teaches others that you will accept their lies too. You owe this to yourself.

DR. SHAYANNA MUNGO

Day 6

Curiosity

Microgoal: _____
_____
_____

Trigger forecast: _____
_____
_____

Your mantra: _____
_____
_____

Where do you see value in yourself today? _____
_____
_____

What skill have you sharpened today? _____
_____
_____

I must develop a new habit of _____so that _____
will benefit from my transformation. Developing this new behavior will enable me to live my ideal day.

Your commitment signature: _____

PS: Lying to yourself teaches others that you will accept their lies too. You owe this to yourself.

Day 7

Curiosity

Microgoal: _____
_____
_____

Trigger forecast: _____
_____
_____

Your mantra: _____
_____
_____

Where do you see value in yourself today? _____
_____
_____

What skill have you sharpened today? _____
_____
_____

I must develop a new habit of _____so that _____
will benefit from my transformation. Developing this new behavior will enable me to live my
ideal day.

Your commitment signature: _____

PS: Lying to yourself teaches others that you will accept their lies too. You owe this to yourself.

Day 8

Curiosity

Microgoal: _____
_____
_____

Trigger forecast: _____
_____
_____

Your mantra: _____
_____
_____

Where do you see value in yourself today? _____
_____
_____

What skill have you sharpened today? _____
_____
_____

I must develop a new habit of _____ so that _____ will benefit from my transformation. Developing this new behavior will enable me to live my ideal day.

Your commitment signature: _____

PS: Lying to yourself teaches others that you will accept their lies too. You owe this to yourself.

Day 9

Curiosity

Microgoal: _____
_____
_____

Trigger forecast: _____
_____
_____

Your mantra: _____
_____
_____

Where do you see value in yourself today? _____
_____
_____

What skill have you sharpened today? _____
_____
_____

I must develop a new habit of _____so that _____
will benefit from my transformation. Developing this new behavior will enable me to live my
ideal day.

Your commitment signature: _____

PS: Lying to yourself teaches others that you will accept their lies too. You owe this to yourself.

DR. SHAYANNA MUNGO

Day 10

Curiosity

Microgoal: _____
_____
_____

Trigger forecast: _____
_____
_____

Your mantra: _____
_____
_____

Where do you see value in yourself today? _____
_____
_____

What skill have you sharpened today? _____
_____
_____

I must develop a new habit of _____so that _____ will benefit from my transformation. Developing this new behavior will enable me to live my ideal day.

Your commitment signature: _____

PS: Lying to yourself teaches others that you will accept their lies too. You owe this to yourself.

Day 11

Curiosity

Microgoal: _____
_____
_____

Trigger forecast: _____
_____
_____

Your mantra: _____
_____
_____

Where do you see value in yourself today? _____
_____
_____

What skill have you sharpened today? _____
_____
_____

I must develop a new habit of _____ so that _____ will benefit from my transformation. Developing this new behavior will enable me to live my ideal day.

Your commitment signature: _____

PS: Lying to yourself teaches others that you will accept their lies too. You owe this to yourself.

DR. SHAYANNA MUNGO

Day 12

Curiosity

Microgoal: _____

_____

_____

Trigger forecast: _____

_____

_____

Your mantra: _____

_____

_____

Where do you see value in yourself today? _____

_____

_____

What skill have you sharpened today? _____

_____

_____

I must develop a new habit of _____ so that _____
will benefit from my transformation. Developing this new behavior will enable me to live my
ideal day.

Your commitment signature: _____

PS: Lying to yourself teaches others that you will accept their lies too. You owe this to yourself.

Day 13

Curiosity

Microgoal: _____
_____
_____

Trigger forecast: _____
_____
_____

Your mantra: _____
_____
_____

Where do you see value in yourself today? _____
_____
_____

What skill have you sharpened today? _____
_____
_____

I must develop a new habit of _____ so that _____
will benefit from my transformation. Developing this new behavior will enable me to live my ideal day.

Your commitment signature: _____

PS: Lying to yourself teaches others that you will accept their lies too. You owe this to yourself.

Day 14

Curiosity

Microgoal: _____

_____

_____

Trigger forecast: _____

_____

_____

Your mantra: _____

_____

_____

Where do you see value in yourself today? _____

_____

_____

What skill have you sharpened today? _____

_____

_____

I must develop a new habit of _____ so that _____ will benefit from my transformation. Developing this new behavior will enable me to live my ideal day.

Your commitment signature: _____

PS: Lying to yourself teaches others that you will accept their lies too. You owe this to yourself.

Day 15

Curiosity

Microgoal: _____
_____
_____

Trigger forecast: _____
_____
_____

Your mantra: _____
_____
_____

Where do you see value in yourself today? _____
_____
_____

What skill have you sharpened today? _____
_____
_____

I must develop a new habit of _____so that _____
will benefit from my transformation. Developing this new behavior will enable me to live my
ideal day.

Your commitment signature: _____

PS: Lying to yourself teaches others that you will accept their lies too. You owe this to yourself.

Day 16

Curiosity

Microgoal: _____
_____
_____

Trigger forecast: _____
_____
_____

Your mantra: _____
_____
_____

Where do you see value in yourself today? _____
_____
_____

What skill have you sharpened today? _____
_____
_____

I must develop a new habit of _____ so that _____
will benefit from my transformation. Developing this new behavior will enable me to live my
ideal day.

Your commitment signature: _____

PS: Lying to yourself teaches others that you will accept their lies too. You owe this to yourself.

Day 17

Curiosity

Microgoal: _____
_____
_____

Trigger forecast: _____
_____
_____

Your mantra: _____
_____
_____

Where do you see value in yourself today? _____
_____
_____

What skill have you sharpened today? _____
_____
_____

I must develop a new habit of _____so that _____
will benefit from my transformation. Developing this new behavior will enable me to live my
ideal day.

Your commitment signature: _____

PS: Lying to yourself teaches others that you will accept their lies too. You owe this to yourself.

Day 18

Curiosity

Microgoal: _____

_____

_____

Trigger forecast: _____

_____

_____

Your mantra: _____

_____

_____

Where do you see value in yourself today? _____

_____

_____

What skill have you sharpened today? _____

_____

_____

I must develop a new habit of _____ so that _____
will benefit from my transformation. Developing this new behavior will enable me to live my
ideal day.

Your commitment signature: _____

PS: Lying to yourself teaches others that you will accept their lies too. You owe this to yourself.

Day 19

Curiosity

Microgoal: _____
_____
_____

Trigger forecast: _____
_____
_____

Your mantra: _____
_____
_____

Where do you see value in yourself today? _____
_____
_____

What skill have you sharpened today? _____
_____
_____

I must develop a new habit of _____so that _____
will benefit from my transformation. Developing this new behavior will enable me to live my ideal day.

Your commitment signature: _____

PS: Lying to yourself teaches others that you will accept their lies too. You owe this to yourself.

DR. SHAYANNA MUNGO

Day 20

Curiosity

Microgoal: _____
_____
_____

Trigger forecast: _____
_____
_____

Your mantra: _____
_____
_____

Where do you see value in yourself today? _____
_____
_____

What skill have you sharpened today? _____
_____
_____

I must develop a new habit of _____ so that _____
will benefit from my transformation. Developing this new behavior will enable me to live my
ideal day.

Your commitment signature: _____

PS: Lying to yourself teaches others that you will accept their lies too. You owe this to yourself.

We're Not Doing This

This journey will awaken some need to change behaviors that you do to yourself or allow others to do to you. Share some boundaries that you could establish so you are enjoying more hours in your day.

Communicating expectations is something that you can do. Think about how strongly you would feel if you were waiting in line and someone just stepped in front of you at the grocery store and put their two items on the counter. Without hesitation, you could speak up.

As you are developing ways to introduce conversation to bring awareness of how you would like to be treated, begin the approach in question form. For example, did you realize XYZ? Do you intend to make me feel XYZ? Is it possible we can try this a different way this time?

Boundary	When I Realized It Wasn't Serving Me Well	Ways I Can Communicate My Expectations
1.		
2.		
3.		
4.		
5.		

Boundaries
(Establish boundaries that reinforce the values to help you with what you want to reinforce.)

availability	lies	time
chores	me time	who the chooser is
driving	phone calls	who the payer is
food vendors	prompt	
late	space	

DR. SHAYANNA MUNGO

This Serves Me Well

Characteristics of Me	When I Realized It Wasn't Serving Me Well	Ways I Can Communicate My Expectations
1.		
2.		
3.		
4.		
5.		
6.		
7.		
8.		
9.		
10.		

Characteristics

awareness	learning	quiet
bold	mindful	resentful
creative	naïve	sassy
friendly	objective	strong
hosting	opportunist	timid
inclusive	patient	understanding
independence	positive	unified
kind	pure	vocal

Reset Your Mind

Reframe activity when you feel like you are struggling to stick to your one-hundred-day microgoal.

How do you see the problem: matter of balance or sacrifice?	
How frequently do you experience the problem?	__ Daily (night/morning) __ Weekly
How intense is the problem for you?	____ Several times a day ____ Makes you want to do nothing ____ Totally embarrassed
Where does the fault lie?	
Who is to blame?	
What's the worst experience with this problem?	
Why have you not solved this yet?	
How can you break down this goal into a smaller one?	
What else will you improve when you keep trying?	
Do you need to identify more resources or leverage your existing resources in a different way?	
What is something similar that you have already accomplished?	

Habit Development Reflections

Boundaries are flexible. This means as you learn more about what you do and do not like, you can modify how you qualify what you let in past your boundaries. Unmanaged boundaries will leave you feeling like being taken advantage of or rejected. Let's take time to celebrate. Below, make a list of what went well. Review the list you created and journal the things that indicate that your boundaries are still serving you well.

Celebrations	Prevention

Your boundaries are conditions that you set to meet your expectations. Your boundaries align with your beliefs or what you tell yourself. How does your boundaries contribute to you actualizing your ideal day?

_____

_____

_____

_____

_____

_____

_____

Day 21

Goal Pursuit

You can choose to continue the microgoal from the first twenty days or choose to push the goal lightly. Dedication to building on what you have already accomplished helps you experience your ideal self.

> "Hard and impossible are defined differently. Just because it's hard does not make it impossible" (Shayanna Mungo)

Microgoal: _____
_____
_____
_____

Trigger forecast: _____
_____
_____
_____

Your quote: _____
_____
_____
_____

I must develop a new habit of _____ so that _____ will benefit from my transformation. Developing this new behavior will enable me to live my ideal day.

Your commitment signature: _____

PS: Lying to yourself teaches others that you will accept their lies too. You owe this to yourself.

DR. SHAYANNA MUNGO

Day 22

Goal Pursuit

Microgoal: _____

_____

_____

_____

Trigger forecast: _____

_____

_____

_____

Your quote: _____

_____

_____

_____

I must develop a new habit of _____so that _____
will benefit from my transformation. Developing this new behavior will enable me to live my
ideal day.

Your commitment signature: _____

PS: Lying to yourself teaches others that you will accept their lies too. You owe this to yourself.

Goal Pursuit

Microgoal: _____
_____
_____
_____

Trigger forecast: _____
_____
_____
_____

Your quote: _____
_____
_____
_____

I must develop a new habit of _____so that _____
will benefit from my transformation. Developing this new behavior will enable me to live my
ideal day.

Your commitment signature: _____

PS: Lying to yourself teaches others that you will accept their lies too. You owe this to yourself.

DR. SHAYANNA MUNGO

Day 24

Goal Pursuit

Microgoal: _____
_____
_____
_____

Trigger forecast: _____
_____
_____
_____

Your quote: _____
_____
_____
_____

I must develop a new habit of _____ so that _____
will benefit from my transformation. Developing this new behavior will enable me to live my
ideal day.

Your commitment signature: _____

PS: Lying to yourself teaches others that you will accept their lies too. You owe this to yourself.

Day 25

Goal Pursuit

Microgoal: _____

_____

_____

_____

Trigger forecast: _____

_____

_____

_____

Your quote: _____

_____

_____

_____

I must develop a new habit of _____ so that _____ will benefit from my transformation. Developing this new behavior will enable me to live my ideal day.

Your commitment signature: _____

PS: Lying to yourself teaches others that you will accept their lies too. You owe this to yourself.

Day 26

Goal Pursuit

Microgoal: _____

_____

_____

_____

Trigger forecast: _____

_____

_____

_____

Your quote: _____

_____

_____

_____

I must develop a new habit of _____so that _____
will benefit from my transformation. Developing this new behavior will enable me to live my
ideal day.

Your commitment signature: _____

PS: Lying to yourself teaches others that you will accept their lies too. You owe this to yourself.

 **Day 27**

Goal Pursuit

Microgoal: _____
_____
_____
_____

Trigger forecast: _____
_____
_____
_____

Your quote: _____
_____
_____
_____

I must develop a new habit of _____so that _____
will benefit from my transformation. Developing this new behavior will enable me to live my
ideal day.

Your commitment signature: _____

PS: Lying to yourself teaches others that you will accept their lies too. You owe this to yourself.

Day 28

Goal Pursuit

Microgoal: _____
_____
_____
_____

Trigger forecast: _____
_____
_____
_____

Your quote: _____
_____
_____
_____

I must develop a new habit of _____so that _____
will benefit from my transformation. Developing this new behavior will enable me to live my
ideal day.

Your commitment signature: _____

PS: Lying to yourself teaches others that you will accept their lies too. You owe this to yourself.

Day 29

Goal Pursuit

Microgoal: _____

_____

_____

_____

Trigger forecast: _____

_____

_____

_____

Your quote: _____

_____

_____

_____

I must develop a new habit of _____ so that _____
will benefit from my transformation. Developing this new behavior will enable me to live my ideal day.

Your commitment signature: _____

PS: Lying to yourself teaches others that you will accept their lies too. You owe this to yourself.

Goal Pursuit

Microgoal: _____
_____
_____
_____

Trigger forecast: _____
_____
_____
_____

Your quote: _____
_____
_____
_____

I must develop a new habit of _____ so that _____
will benefit from my transformation. Developing this new behavior will enable me to live my ideal day.

Your commitment signature: _____

PS: Lying to yourself teaches others that you will accept their lies too. You owe this to yourself.

Day 31

Goal Pursuit

Microgoal: _____
_____
_____
_____

Trigger forecast: _____
_____
_____
_____

Your quote: _____
_____
_____
_____

I must develop a new habit of _____ so that _____ will benefit from my transformation. Developing this new behavior will enable me to live my ideal day.

Your commitment signature: _____

PS: Lying to yourself teaches others that you will accept their lies too. You owe this to yourself.

Day 32

Goal Pursuit

Microgoal: _____

_____

_____

_____

Trigger forecast: _____

_____

_____

_____

Your quote: _____

_____

_____

_____

I must develop a new habit of _____so that _____
will benefit from my transformation. Developing this new behavior will enable me to live my
ideal day.

Your commitment signature: _____

PS: Lying to yourself teaches others that you will accept their lies too. You owe this to yourself.

Day 33

Goal Pursuit

Microgoal: _____

_____

_____

_____

Trigger forecast: _____

_____

_____

_____

Your quote: _____

_____

_____

_____

I must develop a new habit of _____so that _____ will benefit from my transformation. Developing this new behavior will enable me to live my ideal day.

Your commitment signature: _____

PS: Lying to yourself teaches others that you will accept their lies too. You owe this to yourself.

Day 34

Goal Pursuit

Microgoal: _____
_____
_____
_____

Trigger forecast: _____
_____
_____
_____

Your quote: _____
_____
_____
_____

I must develop a new habit of _____ so that _____
will benefit from my transformation. Developing this new behavior will enable me to live my ideal day.

Your commitment signature: _____

PS: Lying to yourself teaches others that you will accept their lies too. You owe this to yourself.

Day 35

Goal Pursuit

Microgoal: _____
_____
_____
_____

Trigger forecast: _____
_____
_____
_____

Your quote: _____
_____
_____
_____

I must develop a new habit of _____ so that _____ will benefit from my transformation. Developing this new behavior will enable me to live my ideal day.

Your commitment signature: _____

PS: Lying to yourself teaches others that you will accept their lies too. You owe this to yourself.

Day 36

Goal Pursuit

Microgoal: _____

_____

_____

_____

Trigger forecast: _____

_____

_____

_____

Your quote: _____

_____

_____

_____

I must develop a new habit of _____ so that _____
will benefit from my transformation. Developing this new behavior will enable me to live my
ideal day.

Your commitment signature: _____

PS: Lying to yourself teaches others that you will accept their lies too. You owe this to yourself.

Day 37

Goal Pursuit

Microgoal: _____
_____
_____
_____

Trigger forecast: _____
_____
_____
_____

Your quote: _____
_____
_____
_____

I must develop a new habit of _____ so that _____ will benefit from my transformation. Developing this new behavior will enable me to live my ideal day.

Your commitment signature: _____

PS: Lying to yourself teaches others that you will accept their lies too. You owe this to yourself.

Day 38

Goal Pursuit

Microgoal: _____

_____

_____

_____

Trigger forecast: _____

_____

_____

_____

Your quote: _____

_____

_____

_____

I must develop a new habit of _____ so that _____ will benefit from my transformation. Developing this new behavior will enable me to live my ideal day.

Your commitment signature: _____

PS: Lying to yourself teaches others that you will accept their lies too. You owe this to yourself.

Day 39

Goal Pursuit

Microgoal: _____

_____

_____

_____

Trigger forecast: _____

_____

_____

_____

Your quote: _____

_____

_____

_____

I must develop a new habit of _____ so that _____ will benefit from my transformation. Developing this new behavior will enable me to live my ideal day.

Your commitment signature: _____

PS: Lying to yourself teaches others that you will accept their lies too. You owe this to yourself.

Day 40

Goal Pursuit

Microgoal: _____

_____

_____

_____

Trigger forecast: _____

_____

_____

_____

Your quote: _____

_____

_____

_____

I must develop a new habit of _____ so that _____ will benefit from my transformation. Developing this new behavior will enable me to live my ideal day.

Your commitment signature: _____

PS: Lying to yourself teaches others that you will accept their lies too. You owe this to yourself.

Boundaries

Boundary	When I Realized It Wasn't Serving Me Well	Ways I Can Communicate My Expectations
1.		
2.		
3.		
4.		
5.		

Boundaries

(Establish boundaries that reinforce the values to help you with what you want to reinforce. If your life was operating off of a remote control, who is pressing play, pause, rewind? Is life playing out at the conditions you want or based on others conditional boundaries? Who benefits from the boundaries you are creating or reinforcing?)

availability

chores

driving

food vendors

late

lies

me time

phone calls

prompt

space

time

who the chooser is

who the payer is

DR. SHAYANNA MUNGO

This Serves Me Well

Characteristics of Me	When I Realized It Wasn't Serving Me Well	Ways I Can Communicate My Expectations
1.		
2.		
3.		
4.		
5.		
6.		
7.		
8.		
9.		
10.		

Characteristics

awareness	learning	quiet
bold	mindful	resentful
creative	naïve	sassy
friendly	objective	strong
hosting	opportunist	timid
inclusive	patient	understanding
independence	positive	unified
kind	pure	vocal

 **Think Out Loud**

What are some challenges that are occupying your mind?

_____

_____

_____

_____

Could the experience be lingering in your mind because your values were challenged?

_____

_____

_____

_____

How could you have encouraged a younger version of yourself with this challenge?

_____

_____

_____

_____

Are you willing to take the advice that you would have given your younger self?

_____

_____

_____

_____

Refer to your support contact list. Enlist someone to support you with thinking of one step to overcome this challenge.

Habit Development Reflections

Boundaries are flexible. This means as you learn more about what you do and do not like, you can modify how you qualify what you let in past your boundaries. Unmanaged boundaries will leave you feeling like being taken advantage of or rejected. Let's take time to celebrate. Below, make a list of what went well. Review the list you created and journal the things that indicate that your boundaries are still serving you well.

Celebrations	Prevention

How will these boundaries contribute to you actualizing your ideal day?

_____

_____

_____

_____

_____

_____

_____

Day 41

Persistence

"Keep your face to the sunshine and you cannot see the shadow" Helen Keller

Your mantra: _____

Trigger forecast: _____
_____
_____

Write down as a reminder why this goal is important to your self-worth.
_____
_____
_____

Who has accomplished a goal like yours? _____
_____
_____

What are some obstacles they overcame? _____
_____
_____

How common are the hurdles you are experiencing? _____
_____
_____

DR. SHAYANNA MUNGO

Persistence

Your mantra: _____

Trigger forecast: _____
_____
_____

Write down as a reminder why this goal is important to your self-worth.
_____
_____
_____

Who has accomplished a goal like yours? _____
_____
_____

What are some obstacles they overcame? _____
_____
_____

How common are the hurdles you are experiencing? _____
_____
_____

Persistence

Your mantra: _____

Trigger forecast: _____
_____
_____

Write down as a reminder why this goal is important to your self-worth.
_____
_____
_____

Who has accomplished a goal like yours? _____
_____
_____

What are some obstacles they overcame? _____
_____
_____

How common are the hurdles you are experiencing? _____
_____
_____

Day 44

Persistence

Your mantra: _____

Trigger forecast: _____
_____
_____

Write down as a reminder why this goal is important to your self-worth.
_____
_____
_____

Who has accomplished a goal like yours? _____
_____
_____

What are some obstacles they overcame? _____
_____
_____

How common are the hurdles you are experiencing? _____
_____
_____

Day 45

Persistence

Your mantra: _____

Trigger forecast: _____
_____
_____

Write down as a reminder why this goal is important to your self-worth.
_____
_____
_____

Who has accomplished a goal like yours? _____
_____
_____

What are some obstacles they overcame? _____
_____
_____

How common are the hurdles you are experiencing? _____
_____
_____

DR. SHAYANNA MUNGO

Day 46

Persistence

Your mantra: _____

Trigger forecast: _____
_____
_____

Write down as a reminder why this goal is important to your self-worth.
_____
_____
_____

Who has accomplished a goal like yours? _____
_____
_____

What are some obstacles they overcame? _____
_____
_____

How common are the hurdles you are experiencing? _____
_____
_____

Day 47

Persistence

Your mantra: _____

Trigger forecast: _____
_____
_____

Write down as a reminder why this goal is important to your self-worth.
_____
_____
_____

Who has accomplished a goal like yours? _____
_____
_____

What are some obstacles they overcame? _____
_____
_____

How common are the hurdles you are experiencing? _____
_____
_____

DR. SHAYANNA MUNGO

Day 48

Persistence

Your mantra: _____

Trigger forecast: _____
_____
_____

Write down as a reminder why this goal is important to your self-worth.
_____
_____
_____

Who has accomplished a goal like yours? _____
_____
_____

What are some obstacles they overcame? _____
_____
_____

How common are the hurdles you are experiencing? _____
_____
_____

Day 49

Persistence

Your mantra: _____

Trigger forecast: _____
_____
_____

Write down as a reminder why this goal is important to your self-worth.
_____
_____
_____

Who has accomplished a goal like yours? _____
_____
_____

What are some obstacles they overcame? _____
_____
_____

How common are the hurdles you are experiencing? _____
_____
_____

Day 50

Persistence

Your mantra: _____

Trigger forecast: _____
_____
_____

Write down as a reminder why this goal is important to your self-worth.
_____
_____
_____

Who has accomplished a goal like yours? _____
_____
_____

What are some obstacles they overcame? _____
_____
_____

How common are the hurdles you are experiencing? _____
_____
_____

Day 51

Persistence

Your mantra: _____

Trigger forecast: _____
_____
_____

Write down as a reminder why this goal is important to your self-worth.
_____
_____
_____

Who has accomplished a goal like yours? _____
_____
_____

What are some obstacles they overcame? _____
_____
_____

How common are the hurdles you are experiencing? _____
_____
_____

DR. SHAYANNA MUNGO

Day 52

Persistence

Your mantra: _____

Trigger forecast: _____
_____
_____

Write down as a reminder why this goal is important to your self-worth.
_____
_____
_____

Who has accomplished a goal like yours? _____
_____
_____

What are some obstacles they overcame? _____
_____
_____

How common are the hurdles you are experiencing? _____
_____
_____

Persistence

Your mantra: _____

Trigger forecast: _____
_____
_____

Write down as a reminder why this goal is important to your self-worth.
_____
_____
_____

Who has accomplished a goal like yours? _____
_____
_____

What are some obstacles they overcame? _____
_____
_____

How common are the hurdles you are experiencing? _____
_____
_____

Day 54

Persistence

Your mantra: _____

Trigger forecast: _____
_____
_____

Write down as a reminder why this goal is important to your self-worth.
_____
_____
_____

Who has accomplished a goal like yours? _____
_____
_____

What are some obstacles they overcame? _____
_____
_____

How common are the hurdles you are experiencing? _____
_____
_____

Persistence

Your mantra: _____

Trigger forecast: _____
_____
_____

Write down as a reminder why this goal is important to your self-worth.
_____
_____
_____

Who has accomplished a goal like yours? _____
_____
_____

What are some obstacles they overcame? _____
_____
_____

How common are the hurdles you are experiencing? _____
_____
_____

Day 56

Persistence

Your mantra: _____

Trigger forecast: _____
_____
_____

Write down as a reminder why this goal is important to your self-worth.
_____
_____
_____

Who has accomplished a goal like yours? _____
_____
_____

What are some obstacles they overcame? _____
_____
_____

How common are the hurdles you are experiencing? _____
_____
_____

Persistence

Your mantra: _____

Trigger forecast: _____
_____
_____

Write down as a reminder why this goal is important to your self-worth.

_____
_____
_____

Who has accomplished a goal like yours? _____
_____
_____

What are some obstacles they overcame? _____
_____
_____

How common are the hurdles you are experiencing? _____
_____
_____

Persistence

Your mantra: _____

Trigger forecast: _____
_____
_____

Write down as a reminder why this goal is important to your self-worth.
_____
_____
_____

Who has accomplished a goal like yours? _____
_____
_____

What are some obstacles they overcame? _____
_____
_____

How common are the hurdles you are experiencing? _____
_____
_____

Persistence

Your mantra: _____

Trigger forecast: _____
_____
_____

Write down as a reminder why this goal is important to your self-worth.
_____
_____
_____

Who has accomplished a goal like yours? _____
_____
_____

What are some obstacles they overcame? _____
_____
_____

How common are the hurdles you are experiencing? _____
_____
_____

Day 60

Persistence

Your mantra: _____

Trigger forecast: _____
_____
_____

Write down as a reminder why this goal is important to your self-worth.
_____
_____
_____

Who has accomplished a goal like yours? _____
_____
_____

What are some obstacles they overcame? _____
_____
_____

How common are the hurdles you are experiencing? _____
_____
_____

Self-Worth Affirmations

Let's identify some affirmations that you can use. These can be helpful as you imagine your ideal self as you are changing your thoughts when you are being tempted by your triggers.

Affirmations to Use	How This Supports My Microgoal
1.	
2.	
3.	
4.	
5.	
6.	
7.	
8.	
9.	
10.	

Affirmations

I am capable.

I am enough.

I am resourceful.

I am resilient.

I am safe.

I am strong.

Habit Development Reflections

Boundaries are flexible. This means as you learn more about what you do and do not like, you can modify how you qualify what you let in past your boundaries. Unmanaged boundaries will leave you feeling like being taken advantage of or rejected. Let's take time to celebrate. Below, make a list of what went well. Review the list you created and journal the things that indicate that your boundaries are still serving you well.

Celebrations	Prevention

How will these boundaries contribute to you actualizing your ideal day?

_____

_____

_____

_____

_____

What patterns are more obvious to you as you are going through this process? Do the patterns have more to do you with changing yourself, being in control of a certain outcome, requiring a certain time to fulfill the change, or changing yourself? You will be most successful with focusing only on changing yourself. The experiences are simply opportunities to mature yourself to reach your ideal self.

Responsibility

"I just got to a point where I decided that I want to life an unbullshitafied life." Steve Maraboli

Your mantra: _____

Trigger forecast: _____
_____
_____

What does it feel like to stay committed to yourself?
_____
_____
_____

Have you noticed if you are sensitive to the conditions of your environment since embarking on this journey? (Sensitivity will increase the more self-aware you are.)
_____
_____
_____

How has your body language or tone of voice changed since working on this goal?
_____
_____
_____

I agree with you to believe that you can master this microgoal.

Day 62

Responsibility

Your mantra: _____

Trigger forecast: _____
_____
_____

What does it feel like to stay committed to yourself?
_____
_____
_____

Have you noticed if you are sensitive to the conditions of your environment since embarking on this journey? (Sensitivity will increase the more self-aware you are.)
_____
_____
_____

How has your body language or tone of voice changed since working on this goal?
_____
_____
_____

I agree with you to believe that you can master this microgoal.

Day 63

Responsibility

Your mantra: _____

Trigger forecast: _____
_____
_____

What does it feel like to stay committed to yourself?
_____
_____
_____

Have you noticed if you are sensitive to the conditions of your environment since embarking on this journey? (Sensitivity will increase the more self-aware you are.)
_____
_____
_____

How has your body language or tone of voice changed since working on this goal?
_____
_____
_____

I agree with you to believe that you can master this microgoal.

Day 64

Responsibility

Your mantra: _____

Trigger forecast: _____

_____

_____

What does it feel like to stay committed to yourself?

_____

_____

_____

Have you noticed if you are sensitive to the conditions of your environment since embarking on this journey? (Sensitivity will increase the more self-aware you are.)

_____

_____

_____

How has your body language or tone of voice changed since working on this goal?

_____

_____

_____

I agree with you to believe that you can master this microgoal.

Day 65

Responsibility

Your mantra: _____

Trigger forecast: _____
_____
_____

What does it feel like to stay committed to yourself?
_____
_____
_____

Have you noticed if you are sensitive to the conditions of your environment since embarking on this journey? (Sensitivity will increase the more self-aware you are.)
_____
_____
_____

How has your body language or tone of voice changed since working on this goal?
_____
_____
_____

I agree with you to believe that you can master this microgoal.

Responsibility

Your mantra: _____

Trigger forecast: _____
_____
_____

What does it feel like to stay committed to yourself?
_____
_____
_____

Have you noticed if you are sensitive to the conditions of your environment since embarking on this journey? (Sensitivity will increase the more self-aware you are.)
_____
_____
_____

How has your body language or tone of voice changed since working on this goal?
_____
_____
_____

I agree with you to believe that you can master this microgoal.

Responsibility

Your mantra: _____

Trigger forecast: _____
_____
_____

What does it feel like to stay committed to yourself?
_____
_____
_____

Have you noticed if you are sensitive to the conditions of your environment since embarking on this journey? (Sensitivity will increase the more self-aware you are.)
_____
_____
_____

How has your body language or tone of voice changed since working on this goal?
_____
_____
_____

I agree with you to believe that you can master this microgoal.

Day 68

Responsibility

Your mantra: _____

Trigger forecast: _____

_____

_____

What does it feel like to stay committed to yourself?

_____

_____

_____

Have you noticed if you are sensitive to the conditions of your environment since embarking on this journey? (Sensitivity will increase the more self-aware you are.)

_____

_____

_____

How has your body language or tone of voice changed since working on this goal?

_____

_____

_____

I agree with you to believe that you can master this microgoal.

Day 69

Responsibility

Your mantra: _____

Trigger forecast: _____
_____
_____

What does it feel like to stay committed to yourself?
_____
_____
_____

Have you noticed if you are sensitive to the conditions of your environment since embarking on this journey? (Sensitivity will increase the more self-aware you are.)
_____
_____
_____

How has your body language or tone of voice changed since working on this goal?
_____
_____
_____

I agree with you to believe that you can master this microgoal.

Day 70

Responsibility

Your mantra: _____

Trigger forecast: _____
_____
_____

What does it feel like to stay committed to yourself?
_____
_____
_____

Have you noticed if you are sensitive to the conditions of your environment since embarking on this journey? (Sensitivity will increase the more self-aware you are.)
_____
_____
_____

How has your body language or tone of voice changed since working on this goal?
_____
_____
_____

I agree with you to believe that you can master this microgoal.

Day 71

Responsibility

Your mantra: _____

Trigger forecast: _____
_____
_____

What does it feel like to stay committed to yourself?
_____
_____
_____

Have you noticed if you are sensitive to the conditions of your environment since embarking on this journey? (Sensitivity will increase the more self-aware you are.)
_____
_____
_____

How has your body language or tone of voice changed since working on this goal?
_____
_____
_____

I agree with you to believe that you can master this microgoal.

DR. SHAYANNA MUNGO

Day 71

Responsibility

Your mantra: _____

Trigger forecast: _____
_____
_____

What does it feel like to stay committed to yourself?
_____
_____
_____

Have you noticed if you are sensitive to the conditions of your environment since embarking on this journey? (Sensitivity will increase the more self-aware you are.)
_____
_____
_____

How has your body language or tone of voice changed since working on this goal?
_____
_____
_____

I agree with you to believe that you can master this microgoal.

Responsibility

Your mantra: _____

Trigger forecast: _____
_____
_____

What does it feel like to stay committed to yourself?
_____
_____
_____

Have you noticed if you are sensitive to the conditions of your environment since embarking on this journey? (Sensitivity will increase the more self-aware you are.)
_____
_____
_____

How has your body language or tone of voice changed since working on this goal?
_____
_____
_____

I agree with you to believe that you can master this microgoal.

DR. SHAYANNA MUNGO

Day 74

Responsibility

Your mantra: _____

Trigger forecast: _____
_____
_____

What does it feel like to stay committed to yourself?
_____
_____
_____

Have you noticed if you are sensitive to the conditions of your environment since embarking on this journey? (Sensitivity will increase the more self-aware you are.)
_____
_____
_____

How has your body language or tone of voice changed since working on this goal?
_____
_____
_____

I agree with you to believe that you can master this microgoal.

Responsibility

Your mantra: _____

Trigger forecast: _____

_____

_____

What does it feel like to stay committed to yourself?

_____

_____

_____

Have you noticed if you are sensitive to the conditions of your environment since embarking on this journey? (Sensitivity will increase the more self-aware you are.)

_____

_____

_____

How has your body language or tone of voice changed since working on this goal?

_____

_____

_____

I agree with you to believe that you can master this microgoal.

DR. SHAYANNA MUNGO

Day 76

Responsibility

Your mantra: _____

Trigger forecast: _____

_____

_____

What does it feel like to stay committed to yourself?

_____

_____

_____

Have you noticed if you are sensitive to the conditions of your environment since embarking on this journey? (Sensitivity will increase the more self-aware you are.)

_____

_____

_____

How has your body language or tone of voice changed since working on this goal?

_____

_____

_____

I agree with you to believe that you can master this microgoal.

Responsibility

Your mantra: _____

Trigger forecast: _____

_____

_____

What does it feel like to stay committed to yourself?

_____

_____

_____

Have you noticed if you are sensitive to the conditions of your environment since embarking on this journey? (Sensitivity will increase the more self-aware you are.)

_____

_____

_____

How has your body language or tone of voice changed since working on this goal?

_____

_____

_____

I agree with you to believe that you can master this microgoal.

Responsibility

Your mantra: _____

Trigger forecast: _____

_____

_____

What does it feel like to stay committed to yourself?

_____

_____

_____

Have you noticed if you are sensitive to the conditions of your environment since embarking on this journey? (Sensitivity will increase the more self-aware you are.)

_____

_____

_____

How has your body language or tone of voice changed since working on this goal?

_____

_____

_____

I agree with you to believe that you can master this microgoal.

Responsibility

Your mantra: _____

Trigger forecast: _____
_____
_____

What does it feel like to stay committed to yourself?
_____
_____
_____

Have you noticed if you are sensitive to the conditions of your environment since embarking on this journey? (Sensitivity will increase the more self-aware you are.)
_____
_____
_____

How has your body language or tone of voice changed since working on this goal?
_____
_____
_____

I agree with you to believe that you can master this microgoal.

Responsibility

Your mantra: _____

Trigger forecast: _____
_____
_____

What does it feel like to stay committed to yourself?
_____
_____
_____

Have you noticed if you are sensitive to the conditions of your environment since embarking on this journey? (Sensitivity will increase the more self-aware you are.)
_____
_____
_____

How has your body language or tone of voice changed since working on this goal?
_____
_____
_____

I agree with you to believe that you can master this microgoal.

Healthy Habits

Retained Habits	When I Realized It Wasn't Serving Me Well	Ways I Can Communicate My Expectations
1.		
2.		
3.		
4.		
5.		
6.		
7.		
8.		
9.		
10.		

Habits

assuming	cleaning	inclusive	shopping
coaching	daring	joking	talking fast
controlling	interrupting	listening	yelling

Change of Habit	When I Realized It Wasn't Serving Me Well	Ways I Can Communicate My Expectations
1.		
2.		
3.		
4.		
5.		
6.		
7.		
8.		
9.		
10.		

DR. SHAYANNA MUNGO

Habit Development Reflections

Boundaries are flexible. This means as you learn more about what you do and do not like, you can modify how you qualify what you let in past your boundaries. Unmanaged boundaries will leave you feeling like being taken advantage of or rejected. Let's take time to celebrate. Below, make a list of what went well. Review the list you created and journal the things that indicate that your boundaries are still serving you well.

Celebrations	Prevention

How will these boundaries contribute to you actualizing your ideal day?

_____

_____

_____

_____

_____

_____

_____

Day 81

Self-Management

"Time is what we want most and what we use worst." William Penn

Your mantra: _____

Trigger forecast: _____
_____
_____

Are you proud of your transformation so far? _____
_____
_____

Who have you shared your growth experience with? _____
_____
_____

I must develop a new habit of _____ so that _____
will benefit from my transformation. Developing this new behavior will enable me to live my ideal day.

Your commitment signature: _____

PS: Lying to yourself teaches others that you will accept their lies too. You owe this to yourself.

Day 82

Self-Management

Your mantra: _____

Trigger forecast: _____
_____
_____

Are you proud of your transformation so far? _____
_____
_____

Who have you shared your growth experience with? _____
_____
_____

I must develop a new habit of _____ so that _____ will benefit from my transformation. Developing this new behavior will enable me to live my ideal day.

Your commitment signature: _____

PS: Lying to yourself teaches others that you will accept their lies too. You owe this to yourself.

Day 83

Self-Management

Your mantra: _____

Trigger forecast: _____
_____
_____

Are you proud of your transformation so far? _____
_____
_____

Who have you shared your growth experience with? _____
_____
_____

I must develop a new habit of _____ so that _____
will benefit from my transformation. Developing this new behavior will enable me to live my
ideal day.

Your commitment signature: _____

PS: Lying to yourself teaches others that you will accept their lies too. You owe this to yourself.

Day 84

Self-Management

Your mantra: _____

Trigger forecast: _____
_____
_____

Are you proud of your transformation so far? _____
_____
_____

Who have you shared your growth experience with? _____
_____
_____

I must develop a new habit of _____ so that _____
will benefit from my transformation. Developing this new behavior will enable me to live my
ideal day.

Your commitment signature: _____

PS: Lying to yourself teaches others that you will accept their lies too. You owe this to yourself.

Day 85

Self-Management

Your mantra: _____

Trigger forecast: _____
_____
_____

Are you proud of your transformation so far? _____
_____
_____

Who have you shared your growth experience with? _____
_____
_____

I must develop a new habit of _____ so that _____
will benefit from my transformation. Developing this new behavior will enable me to live my ideal day.

Your commitment signature: _____

PS: Lying to yourself teaches others that you will accept their lies too. You owe this to yourself.

Day 86

Self-Management

Your mantra: _____

Trigger forecast: _____
_____
_____

Are you proud of your transformation so far? _____
_____
_____

Who have you shared your growth experience with? _____
_____
_____

I must develop a new habit of _____ so that _____
will benefit from my transformation. Developing this new behavior will enable me to live my
ideal day.

Your commitment signature: _____

PS: Lying to yourself teaches others that you will accept their lies too. You owe this to yourself.

Day 87

Self-Management

Your mantra: _____

Trigger forecast: _____
_____
_____

Are you proud of your transformation so far? _____
_____
_____

Who have you shared your growth experience with? _____
_____
_____

I must develop a new habit of _____ so that _____ will benefit from my transformation. Developing this new behavior will enable me to live my ideal day.

Your commitment signature: _____

PS: Lying to yourself teaches others that you will accept their lies too. You owe this to yourself.

Day 88

Self-Management

Your mantra: _____

Trigger forecast: _____
_____
_____

Are you proud of your transformation so far? _____
_____
_____

Who have you shared your growth experience with? _____
_____
_____

I must develop a new habit of _____ so that _____
will benefit from my transformation. Developing this new behavior will enable me to live my ideal day.

Your commitment signature: _____

PS: Lying to yourself teaches others that you will accept their lies too. You owe this to yourself.

Day 89

Self-Management

Your mantra: _____

Trigger forecast: _____
_____
_____

Are you proud of your transformation so far? _____
_____
_____

Who have you shared your growth experience with? _____
_____
_____

I must develop a new habit of _____ so that _____
will benefit from my transformation. Developing this new behavior will enable me to live my ideal day.

Your commitment signature: _____

PS: Lying to yourself teaches others that you will accept their lies too. You owe this to yourself.

DR. SHAYANNA MUNGO

Day 90

Self-Management

Your mantra: _____

Trigger forecast: _____
_____
_____

Are you proud of your transformation so far? _____
_____
_____

Who have you shared your growth experience with? _____
_____
_____

I must develop a new habit of _____ so that _____
will benefit from my transformation. Developing this new behavior will enable me to live my
ideal day.

Your commitment signature: _____

PS: Lying to yourself teaches others that you will accept their lies too. You owe this to yourself.

Day 91

Self-Management

Your mantra: _____

Trigger forecast: _____
_____
_____

Are you proud of your transformation so far? _____
_____
_____

Who have you shared your growth experience with? _____
_____
_____

I must develop a new habit of _____ so that _____
will benefit from my transformation. Developing this new behavior will enable me to live my
ideal day.

Your commitment signature: _____

PS: Lying to yourself teaches others that you will accept their lies too. You owe this to yourself.

DR. SHAYANNA MUNGO

Day 92

Self-Management

Your mantra: _____

Trigger forecast: _____
_____
_____

Are you proud of your transformation so far? _____
_____
_____

Who have you shared your growth experience with? _____
_____
_____

I must develop a new habit of _____ so that _____
will benefit from my transformation. Developing this new behavior will enable me to live my
ideal day.

Your commitment signature: _____

PS: Lying to yourself teaches others that you will accept their lies too. You owe this to yourself.

Day 93

Self-Management

Your mantra: _____

Trigger forecast: _____
_____
_____

Are you proud of your transformation so far? _____
_____
_____

Who have you shared your growth experience with? _____
_____
_____

I must develop a new habit of _____ so that _____
will benefit from my transformation. Developing this new behavior will enable me to live my
ideal day.

Your commitment signature: _____

PS: Lying to yourself teaches others that you will accept their lies too. You owe this to yourself.

DR. SHAYANNA MUNGO

Day 94

Self-Management

Your mantra: _____

Trigger forecast: _____
_____
_____

Are you proud of your transformation so far? _____
_____
_____

Who have you shared your growth experience with? _____
_____
_____

I must develop a new habit of _____ so that _____
will benefit from my transformation. Developing this new behavior will enable me to live my ideal day.

Your commitment signature: _____

PS: Lying to yourself teaches others that you will accept their lies too. You owe this to yourself.

Day 95

Self-Management

Your mantra: _____

Trigger forecast: _____
_____
_____

Are you proud of your transformation so far? _____
_____
_____

Who have you shared your growth experience with? _____
_____
_____

I must develop a new habit of _____ so that _____
will benefit from my transformation. Developing this new behavior will enable me to live my
ideal day.

Your commitment signature: _____

PS: Lying to yourself teaches others that you will accept their lies too. You owe this to yourself.

DR. SHAYANNA MUNGO

Day 96

Self-Management

Your mantra: _____

Trigger forecast: _____
_____
_____

Are you proud of your transformation so far? _____
_____
_____

Who have you shared your growth experience with? _____
_____
_____

I must develop a new habit of _____ so that _____
will benefit from my transformation. Developing this new behavior will enable me to live my
ideal day.

Your commitment signature: _____

PS: Lying to yourself teaches others that you will accept their lies too. You owe this to yourself.

Self-Management

Your mantra: _____

Trigger forecast: _____
_____
_____

Are you proud of your transformation so far? _____
_____
_____

Who have you shared your growth experience with? _____
_____
_____

I must develop a new habit of _____ so that _____ will benefit from my transformation. Developing this new behavior will enable me to live my ideal day.

Your commitment signature: _____

PS: Lying to yourself teaches others that you will accept their lies too. You owe this to yourself.

DR. SHAYANNA MUNGO

Day 98

Self-Management

Your mantra: _____

Trigger forecast: _____
_____
_____

Are you proud of your transformation so far? _____
_____
_____

Who have you shared your growth experience with? _____
_____
_____

I must develop a new habit of _____ so that _____
will benefit from my transformation. Developing this new behavior will enable me to live my ideal day.

Your commitment signature: _____

PS: Lying to yourself teaches others that you will accept their lies too. You owe this to yourself.

Day 99

Self-Management

Your mantra: _____

Trigger forecast: _____
_____
_____

Are you proud of your transformation so far? _____
_____
_____

Who have you shared your growth experience with? _____
_____
_____

I must develop a new habit of _____ so that _____
will benefit from my transformation. Developing this new behavior will enable me to live my ideal day.

Your commitment signature: _____

PS: Lying to yourself teaches others that you will accept their lies too. You owe this to yourself.

Day 100

Self-Management

Your mantra: _____

Trigger forecast: _____
_____
_____

Are you proud of your transformation so far? _____
_____
_____

Who have you shared your growth experience with? _____
_____
_____

I must develop a new habit of _____so that _____
will benefit from my transformation. Developing this new behavior will enable me to live my
ideal day.

Your commitment signature: _____

PS: Lying to yourself teaches others that you will accept their lies too. You owe this to yourself.

Looking Ahead

What skills did you develop to accomplish the goal?

☐ problem-solving	☐ ability to plan
☐ exercising choice	☐ finding time for self
☐ responding to problems	☐ ability to avoid danger
☐ setting boundaries	☐ other _____
☐ reinforcing boundaries	☐ other _____

Which skills align to reinforcing your new core values?

_____

_____

_____

Self-Actualization

How has this experience prepared you for your next microgoal?

Picture or Description of Your Current Self	Picture or Description of Your Ideal Self

Picture of Actualized Self

Remember, the only person who must believe something is possible is YOU. Not everyone will share your vision.
Do your research to learn from the lessons of others and offer contributions for others to build on.

Repeat these exercises to accomplish your next microgoal. Remove the pressure you put on yourself as to enjoy how you are maturing. "One cannot be prepared for something while secretly believing it will not happen." Nelson Mandela.

Tell Me More

I have shared with you tools that have helped me develop personally and professionally. My desire is that you too will benefit from the exercises.

I grow from feedback and I appreciate you in advance for taking your time to share your success with me. Leave a review with #Goals2Victory

- Google
- LinkedIn
- Amazon
- Twitter

Printed in the United States
by Baker & Taylor Publisher Services